Festivals

My Christmas

Monica Hughes

Heinemann
LIBRARY

Little Nippers

www.heinemann.co.uk/library
Visit our website to find out more information about **Heinemann Library** books.

To order:
☎ Phone 44 (0) 1865 888066
🖹 Send a fax to 44 (0) 1865 314091
💻 Visit the Heinemann Bookshop at www.heinemann.co.uk/library to browse our catalogue and order online.

First published in Great Britain by Heinemann Library, Halley Court, Jordan Hill, Oxford OX2 8EJ, part of Harcourt Education. Heinemann is a registered trademark of Harcourt Education Ltd.

Editorial: Sarah Eason and Georga Godwin
Design: Jo Hinton-Malivoire and Tokay, Bicester, UK (www.tokay.co.uk)
Picture Research: Rosie Garai
Production: Séverine Ribierre

Originated by Dot Gradations Ltd
Printed and bound in China by South China Printing Company

ISBN 978 0 431 18632 0 (hardback)
ISBN 0 431 18632 4 (hardback)
07 06 05 04 03
10 9 8 7 6 5 4 3 2 1

ISBN 978 0 431 18638 2 (paperback)
ISBN 0 431 186383 (paperback)
07 06
10 9 8 7 6 5 4 3

British Library Cataloguing in Publication Data
Hughes, Monica
Little Nippers Festivals My Christmas
263.9'15
A full catalogue record for this book is available from the British Library.

Acknowledgements
The Publishers would like to thank Chris Schwarz and Andes Press Agency p. **8**; Corbis **p. 16** for permission to reproduce photographs.

Cover photograph of the children in costumes, reproduced with permission of Chris Schwarz.

The Publishers would like to thank the family and school involved and Philip Emmett for their assistance in the preparation of this book.

Every effort has been made to contact copyright holders of any material reproduced in this book. Any omissions will be rectified in subsequent printings if notice is given to the Publishers.

Contents

Advent calendars

At Advent we look forward
to Christmas!

We count the days on our Advent calendar

At school

It is fun getting ready for Christmas at school.

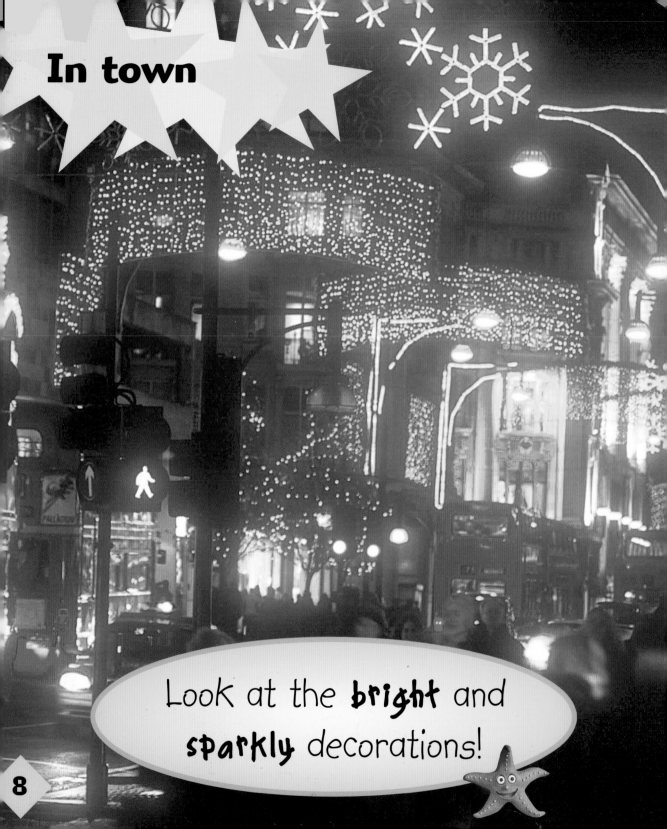

In town

Look at the **bright** and **sparkly** decorations!

Jesus helped people.
We give money to help others too.

Our Christmas tree

I help Daddy
to choose the
right tree.

Then we all decorate it together.

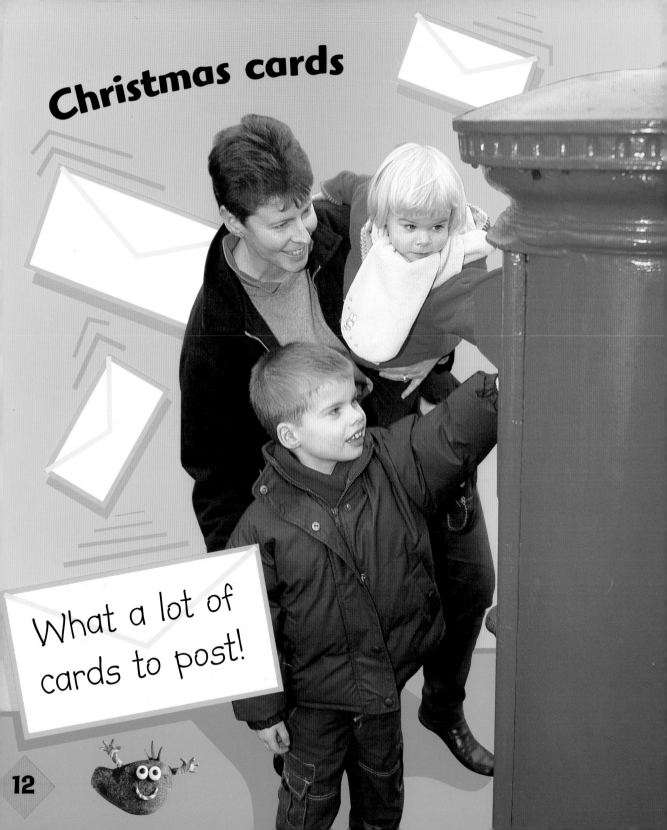

Christmas cards

What a lot of cards to post!

Let's put our cards on show.
Look how pretty they are!

At church

We give presents for children who don't have any.

At church we hear the story of Jesus' birth.

Father Christmas

Look! There's Father Christmas in his grotto.

Presents

This is for you,
Mummy.
Happy Christmas!

Christmas dinner

We eat lots of special, delicious food for our meal.

Christmas fun

It's teatime – yum! Christmas cake and mince pies.

After tea we all play a game.
It's been a perfect Christmas Day!

Index

The end

Notes for adults

Most festivals and celebrations share common elements that will be familiar to the young child, such as new clothes, special food, sending and receiving cards and presents, giving to charity, being with family and friends and a busy and exciting build-up time. It is important that the child has an opportunity to compare and contrast their own experiences with those of the children in the book. This will be helped by asking the child open-ended questions, using phrases like: What do you remember about …? What did we do …? Where did we go …? Who did we see …? How did you feel …?

Christmas is a Christian festival but it has become so commercial that it is observed by many other people. Christmas Day is 25 December and the festival ends twelve days later on 6 January. Special services are held in churches and chapels where the birth of Jesus is recalled, prayers are said and special carols sung. There are many and various customs associated with the festival and these vary from family to family and from country to country throughout the world.

Follow up activities could include finding a children's version of the story of the first Christmas, collecting used Christmas cards and sorting them into different types, for example religious and non religious, and making a list of all the special Christmas things that can be seen around the places where the children live.